EARLY FLYING MACHINES

DISCOVERIES AND INVENTIONS

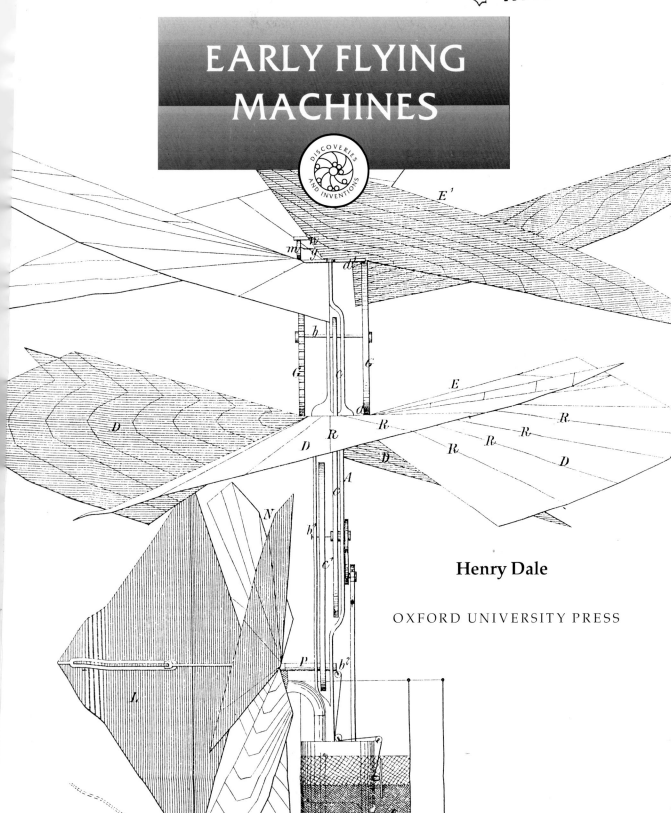

Henry Dale

OXFORD UNIVERSITY PRESS

Inside front cover **Gaston Tissandier, 1867.**

Title page **A drawing from Ponton d'Amécourt's patent for a model helicopter of 1861 (No. 1929).**

This page **George Pocock's man-lifting kite performing a rescue from a shipwreck. Pocock also experimented with the use of kites to pull carriages.**

Photographic acknowledgments

All illustrations in this book have been taken from out-of-copyright material held in the British Library's collections, with the exception of those which carry a credit line in the accompanying caption. Patents are numbered and dated for ease of reference.

OXFORD UNIVERSITY PRESS

Oxford New York Toronto
Delhi Bombay Calcutta Madras Karachi
Kuala Lumpur Singapore Hong Kong Tokyo
Nairobi Dar es Salaam Cape Town
Melbourne Auckland Madrid
and associated companies in
Berlin Ibadan

Copyright © 1992 Henry Dale

First published in 1992 by The British Library. First published in North and South America by Oxford University Press, Inc., 200 Madison Avenue, New York, New York 10016, by arrangement with The British Library

Library of Congress Cataloging in Publication Data

Dale, Henry.
  Early flying machines / Henry Dale.
    p.64, 24.6 x18.9 cm. – (Discoveries and inventions)
  Includes bibliographical references (p.63) and index.
  Summary: Surveys the early history of flight, from the first recorded history of man's attempt to fly to the successful flight of the Wright brothers.
  ISBN 0-19-520966-4 (acid-free paper)
  1. Aeronautics – History – Juvenile literature. [1. Aeronautics – History. 2. Airplanes – History. 3. Flying machines – History.] I. Title. II. Series.
TL547.D16 1992
629. 13'09 – dc20   92-21664
                                                      CIP
                                                       AC

ISBN 0-19-520970-2 (paperback)
ISBN 0-19-520966-4 (hardback)

Printing (last digit) 9 8 7 6 5 4 3 2 1

Designed and set on Ventura in Palatino by Roger Davies
Printed in Singapore

Contents

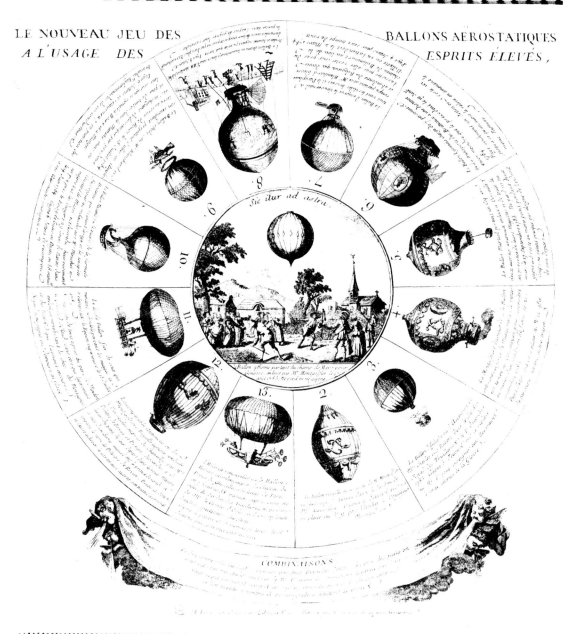

Introduction

What makes people want to fly? Nowadays there are many reasons: to travel on business; to go on holiday; for pleasure; to do research; for education; even to drop bombs on other people on occasions. But it hasn't always been so. At the beginning of this century no one had ever made a controlled powered flight and so none of the modern reasons for flying had been invented. In those days, it seems, people wanted to fly – rather as a mountaineer climbs new routes – because it's a challenge. Something to be done that no one has ever done before; and for self-aggrandizement and profit. But what of the first aeronautical experimenters, as they plummeted ineffectually from their high towers to the waiting ground with their inadequate wings strapped to their inadequate arms? For them the motivation to fly must have been wanting to have the advantages of birds; birds had the ability to soar free of the shackles of the ground, and they wanted to do the same. How glorious it would be to see the world from on high, to swoop and soar, to cross wide valleys and great mountains without effort.

The development of flight followed three strands. First there were the lighter-than-air craft such as balloons and airships which were successful from their modern conception in 1783 by the Montgolfier brothers and J A C Charles. Then there were the attempts by people who thought little about the theory of flight and who invariably failed – though the more money they had, the more magnificent were their failures. Finally there were the intelligent, methodical experimenters who sought to apply science and their continually-expanding knowledge to solving the problems of flight. There were failures for all these

people, and for some their failure led to death. But those who applied science were on the right lines, their efforts contributing to a growing body of knowledge that led to the Wright brothers making their historic powered flights on 17 December 1903. The Wrights succeeded because of all the experimenters who went before them Cayley, Henson, Hargrave, Lilienthal and Chanute to name but five. Early flying machines were often failures, but each of them showed where promising ideas lay or, alternatively, where the approach was not going to come to anything. The Wrights were able to draw on the experience of many people and, as part of a worldwide research and development effort, flew the first successful powered machine.

Even though many inventors swapped ideas and accounts of their work, some were possessive of their knowledge, perhaps seeking immortality by being the first to fly. As Lawrence Hargrave, an Australian engineer who built powered flying models and kites, said: 'Workers must root out the idea that by keeping the results of their labours to themselves a fortune will be assured to them. Patent fees are so much wasted money. The flying machine of the future will not be born fully fledged and capable of flight for 1,000 miles or so. Like everything else it must be evolved gradually. The first difficulty is to get a thing that will fly at all. When this is made, a full description should be published as an aid to others. Excellence of design and workmanship will always defy competition.' Fine though those words were, the reality was – and still is – that if someone felt close to achieving a 'first', he wanted to be the one to do it first, and no one else was going to be helped to beat him to the goal.

An early illustration detailing the ballooning successes in France, where their use was pioneered.

Ancient Dreams

All books about the history of flight begin with the legends that involve flying men and flying machines. There is no reason to suppose that people were any the less keen on trying to fly several thousand years ago than they were in the 19th century. The difference is that their experiments are very much less well documented. The result is that many legends have developed around early would-be aeronauts and their machines where probably the truth was at best a dismal failure, and at worst that of the fearless individual plunging to his death, performing a pointless self-sacrifice on the altar of continuing ignorance. The sad part was that nobody of knowledge was built up about these futile attempts at flight and so they continued for many hundreds of years until it began to dawn on people that there must be more to flying than strapping on a pair of home-made wings and leaping from a tower.

One of the oldest and best-known legends of flight is that of Dædalus and Icarus, which may well contain a grain of truth. Dædalus had made two pairs of wings with feathers and wax with which he and his son Icarus were going to escape from King Minos's labyrinth at Crete. During the flight, Icarus went too close to the sun, the wax melted and his wings disintegrated, whereupon he plummeted to his death in the Aegean Sea. Dædalus continued his escape, eventually landing at Cumæ. It is conceivable that Icarus tried to fly from Crete wearing a pair of wings, and plunged straight to his death. Dædalus, who is credited with inventing the sail, may then have effected his escape by boat. Over the centuries, storytellers would fabricate and embellish the legend.

Around 400 BC Archytas, a philosopher from Taranto, is said to have made a wooden pigeon which flew 'by a mechanism of balancing weights and the breath of a mysterious spirit hidden within it'. It is said elsewhere that his model was propelled by a jet of steam. Given the state of engineering in those days,

and the availability of tools and materials, it seems unlikely that this flying model bird could have taken to the air, and that if it existed at all it probably did no more than hiss and spit and perhaps bounce about a bit on the floor.

This amply demonstrates the problem with these old stories of flight – there is no real contemporary evidence to support the claims, and there is a wealth of modern knowledge with which to dispute them.

There are many other stories with a ring of truth about them wherein someone tries – and sooner or later fails – to fly with the aid of wings: the mythical King Bladud, dashed to pieces while trying to fly; Saracen of Constantinople who dived from a tower attempting to impress a large crowd with his flying prowess aided by nought but a large garment stiffened with rods; Oliver, a monk of Malmesbury who, with his Dædalus-like wings, tried to fly from a tower, with inevitable results; Giovanni Baptisti Danti who flew around at a wedding until one of his wings broke and he crashed on to the roof of a church – and so on. What all these stories show above all else is that mankind has

Icarus falling to his death, his wings having disintegrated when he flew too close to the sun.

Early ideas for human flight included various methods for harnessing birds.

desired to fly for thousands of years, but took a long time to realize the dream because enthusiasm far out-ran scientific knowledge. The 13th-century scientist and philosopher Roger Bacon was one of the earliest to record thoughts about flight; he wrote that one day there would be flying machines powered by a man sitting in the middle and 'turning some mechanism'. However, he seems to have done no practical work and contributed little of value to the subject.

It was not until Leonardo da Vinci (1452–1519) that we begin to see the considered scientific study of flight. He left behind a wealth of drawings and writing to support his ideas – there is no doubt that *he* existed, and there is no doubt that he thought about the subject at a greater depth than had been done before. In his treatise on the flight of birds he wrote that, since a bird

is an instrument working according to the laws of mathematics, and that since man is capable of building an exact copy of such an instrument complete except for the muscle power of the bird, it should be possible, by replacing the bird's muscles with those of a man, to create a powered flying machine. He thought that since large birds expend little energy when they fly (presumably because they are soaring on rising currents of hot air) it should be within man's muscular capacity to do the same thing. He was not far wrong as we now see hang-gliders – which are equivalent to Leonardo's 'instrument' being piloted by people expending relatively little energy while flying in thermals. Of course that is not what he had in mind, but that is how it has worked out.

Along with his designs for man-powered ornithopters (machines with flapping wings), Leonardo had other ideas – a lifting screw which, if turned fast enough, would wind itself into the air, and a parachute – though he seems never to have tried them himself.

In 1670, Francesco Lana a mathematician, scientist and Jesuit who had taken vows of poverty, designed a flying machine based on the fact that air has weight. He wanted to make four huge copper spheres and evacuate the air from them by means of a column of water: if the spheres were full of water, and attached to water-filled pipes whose other ends were immersed in water 34 feet below, opening a tap would allow the water to drain from the sphere, leaving a vacuum. The tap would then be closed. These spheres would be attached to a ship which would be lifted into the air by their buoyancy. The trouble with this idea was that air pressure would have collapsed the spheres long before they became buoyant. But Lana was never to know that: because of his vows of poverty, he didn't have the cash to test his ideas. He proposed to propel his craft by oars which would row against the air. He described how this ship could be used to fly over cities and drop bombs but, being a religious man, he thought that God would never allow such a machine to be successful.

Some time between 1675 and 1680 Besnier, a locksmith of Sablé, constructed a flying machine with which it is said he made some successful gliding flights. According to contemporary records he was able to cross a river of considerable width before coming to earth. Looking at the picture of his apparatus, it is hard to believe this story: not only are the 'flappers' much smaller than they would need to be, but the pilot is naked – unlikely for someone experimenting with flight, presumably on a hillside covered with rocks and thistles. Maybe some slight hop into the air was converted by way of a series of retellings into the story of these flights.

After Leonardo, the next great thinker on the subject was Borelli who concluded in 1680, after much thought and study of bird flight, that 'It is impossible that men should be able to fly craftily by their own strength'. He was not to be proved wrong for some 300 years when the *Gossamer Condor* made its début in 1977.

Some say that Borelli's learned conclusion stifled

Leonardo da Vinci's sketch for a mechanical bird with powered wings and tail.

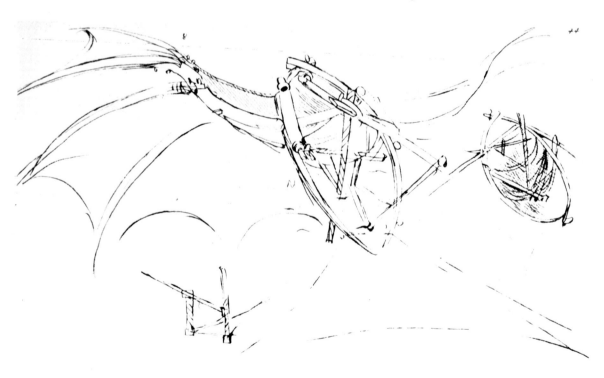

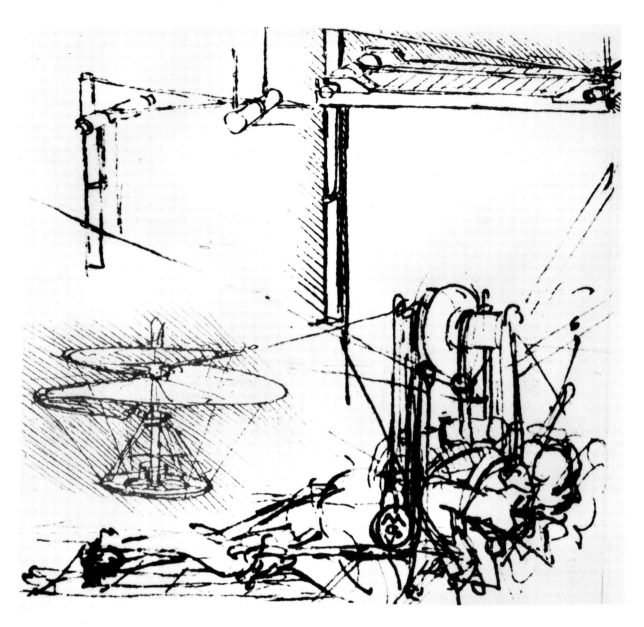

**Leonardo da Vinci's helicopter, with detail of
apparatus for harnessing human power to drive it.**

experimentation with any heavier-than-air apparatus
until well into the 19th century. This is hard to believe
since there were many people who experimented with
heavier-than-air flight (some to their cost). Only those
wealthy and learned enough would have had access to
Borelli's writing people such as Sir George Cayley
(1773–1857) who, if he read it, wasn't put off by it.
Borelli did not delay development of heavier-than-air
flight, but merely pointed it away from the futile appli-
cation of human power.

Francesco Lana's flying machine supported by buoyant copper spheres. Details at top left and right show how Lana proposed to evacuate the air from the spheres using water and a tube 34 feet long.

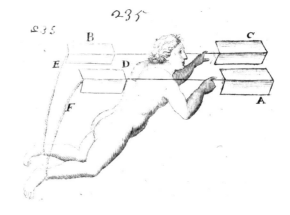

Besnier's flying apparatus, powered by arms and legs, must have been particularly uncomfortable to use in the nude.

Balloons

No one knows who was the first to propound the idea of the hot-air balloon. Since the discovery of fire, observant individuals must have noticed smoke and sparks rising from the flames and dreamed of harnessing this flying property. At the beginning of the 18th century a Brazilian monk, Bartholomeu Lourenço de Gusmão, is said to have experimented with some kind of flying machine that was raised by fire. One story is that he flew a model hot-air balloon indoors at the Casa da India, Terreiro do Paço, Portugal on 8 August 1709. No definite records exist of such a hot-air balloon; an unlikely omission if he had been successful.

It was not until 1766 that the first definite steps towards lighter-than-air flight were taken when the reclusive English physicist Henry Cavendish (1731–1810) discovered hydrogen gas and showed it to be less dense than air. Dr Joseph Black (1728–1799) of Edinburgh claimed some time later that in 1777 or 1778

The flying machine of Bartholomeu Lourenço de Gusmão which was supposedly demonstrated to the King of Portugal in 1709.

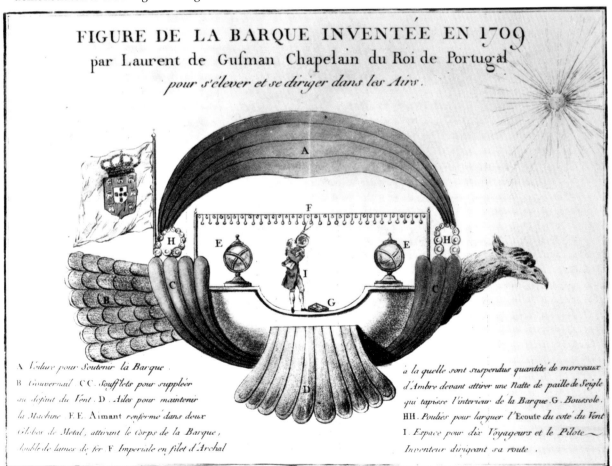

he discussed with friends the possibility of filling a vessel with hydrogen in order to raise it into the air and therefore claimed for himself the invention of the gas balloon. Leo Cavallo experimented with soap bubbles filled with hydrogen gas – obviously these rose in the air and he soon had ideas for filling bladders with the gas. Unfortunately for him the gas escaped through the pores in the bladders.

Eventually hot-air and hydrogen balloons were developed in parallel, by different people, and made their débuts in the same year.

The Montgolfier Brothers, Joseph (1740–1810) and Etienne (1745–1799), are generally recognized as the inventors of the hot-air balloon – though who knows what influence earlier ideas had on them? As with all inventions, the balloon was the result of interactions of different people's thoughts and ideas. It is said that a silk garment drying above an oven had turned their thoughts to the subject of flight when they noticed how it tended to lift in the hot air. The Montgolfier brothers were the sons of a paper maker, and both were scientifically minded as well as being practically skilled. They were keen to try the idea that air from the upper atmosphere had some lighter property than the air at ground level. This theory seemed to be borne out by the way clouds rose up. They had the idea of filling a vessel – perhaps a paper bag – with steam to simulate a cloud. Sure enough, the bag rose. In 1782, Joseph had the idea of using the apparent lifting power of smoke as a substitute for steam since they looked similar and both rose from a source of heat. He constructed a small balloon from some old fabric and lit a fire under it. It ascended to the ceiling. He and Etienne conducted further balloon experiments and, in June 1783, invited the Representative Assembly of Vivarais, gathered in Annonay, to witness the ascent of their new invention from one of the town squares. The balloon was 35 feet (10.7 m) in diameter, made of sections of fabric reinforced with paper buttoned together. Beneath its open bottom hung a burner containing a fire of straw and wool producing hot air which caused it to rise rapidly and to a great height. After ten minutes it came down and the burner set fire to the balloon.

There was an immediate enthusiasm for the new invention; it was reported widely, and the brothers were invited to the Academy of Science in Paris to repeat their demonstration. There was talk of it being used as a new form of transport, and opening up a whole new vista of scientific discovery.

Meanwhile in Paris the physicist Dr Jacques Alexandre César Charles (1746–1823) had undertaken to demonstrate another kind of balloon – one filled with hydrogen. Charles had observed the lifting power of hot air and reasoned that hydrogen had even greater lifting power. He solved the problem of the gas escaping through the pores of a gas bladder with the help of two instrument makers, the Robert brothers, who had discovered a solvent for rubber. They constructed a balloon of silk 13 feet in diameter, made impermeable to gas by varnishing it with the dissolved rubber. They filled the envelope through lead pipes by adding sulphuric acid to iron filings which, in the process of oxidizing the iron, produced great quantities of hydrogen gas. It needed about a quarter of a ton of acid and half a ton of iron, and the balloon took four days to fill. It was then taken to the Champs de Mars and released on 27 August 1783 in front of a crowd; it rose rapidly and disappeared to the north-east. It flew for about 45 minutes before coming down about 15 miles (24 km) from its release point. It had risen so high that the expanding gas within it had torn the envelope; it had sunk back to earth at the village of Gonesse whose inhabitants attacked it, thinking it to be some sort of devil, hacking at it with rakes and hoes before dragging it around behind a horse until it was completely destroyed.

Etienne Montgolfier built a 42-foot (12.8 m) diameter linen balloon coated with paper which was destroyed by wind and rain before he could launch it. He built another made from waterproof linen and launched it before a crowd on 19 September 1783 at Versailles. Under it was a basket containing a sheep, a cockerel and a duck, an experiment to see if animals could exist away from the ground. The balloon was torn at lift-off and so flew only for eight minutes, landing about two miles away. The sheep and the duck were unharmed, but the cock was injured. Some know-all attributed this to the harmful effect of the rarefied atmosphere before it was discovered that the sheep had trodden on

The first public demonstration of a hot-air balloon by the Montgolfier brothers on 5 June 1783 at Annonay, France. There appear to have been remarkably few spectators for such an historic event.

its wing. The trial was considered successful enough to build a man-carrying balloon.

Etienne Montgolfier built an enlarged version of his Versailles balloon 70 feet (21.3 m) in height and 46 feet (14 m) in diameter, and added a circular gallery in which people could stand. The inside of the gallery was fixed to a ring at the base of the balloon and its outer part was supported by ropes. A burner weighing 1600 pounds (726 kg) was suspended from chains inside the balloon; it could be tended from the gallery through two holes in the fabric opposite one another. During tethered experiments, François Pilâtre de Rozier, a physicist and chemist, made captive ascents to as high as 324 feet (99 m), on some occasions accompanied by distinguished guests.

For the free man-carrying ascent it had been intended to send aloft two criminals who had been condemned to death, with the incentive that if they survived they would be released. However, the King of France was persuaded to allow de Rozier and a friend go instead. (What happened to the criminals is not clear.) On 21 November 1783, de Rozier and François Laurent – the Marquis d'Arlandes – an infantry major, rose from Château de la Muette at the edge of the Bois de Boulogne in Paris on the first-ever manned non-tethered balloon flight. They had to work hard feeding straw into the burner to keep the fire alight and prevent them from sinking to earth. They could not actually see one another because they had to remain counterbalanced on opposite sides of the gallery. Words were exchanged more than once because d'Arlandes kept breaking off to enjoy the view while de Rozier was working flat out stoking the fire to keep the balloon aloft. The flight lasted 25 minutes, being brought to a premature end when d'Arlandes noticed that the gallery was breaking up, and they were in mortal danger. They had flown over six miles (10 km) and had risen to over 3,000 feet (914 m). When they landed they still had two-thirds of the straw left.

The hydrogen balloon developed in parallel with the hot-air balloon. After his successful model demonstration, Charles built a full-size hydrogen balloon 26 feet (7.9 m) in diameter. It had a fabric envelope coated with elastic gum and a net over the top which was attached to a wooden ring running round the middle of the balloon from which was suspended a basket. In this Charles and one of the Robert brothers took off from the Tuileries on 1 December 1783. They seem to have been much better prepared than the hot-air balloonists, and enjoyed a completely trouble-free flight of two hours five minutes, presumably with ample time for both to enjoy the view. They landed at Nesles where Robert alighted. Though it was getting dark, Charles made a further 35-minute solo flight during

The first balloon passengers a sheep, a cockerel and a duck ascending on 19 September 1783 from Versailles.

which he rose to a height which enabled him to enjoy a second sunset.

A French engineer, Jean-Pierre Blanchard (1753-1809), who had been building a flying machine since 1781, immediately incorporated a hydrogen balloon into his design. Underneath it, he fitted part of his earlier model: a boat with a rudder and two pairs of hinged paddles which alternately opened and closed as they swept back and forth. Between the balloon and the boat was a safety parachute. Blanchard tried his machine out on 2 March 1784 but just before he took off Dupont du Chambon, a pupil from the Military School, tried to climb aboard. In the scuffle he drew his sword, wounded Blanchard on the wrist and cut the parachute and paddles. Blanchard went ahead with the flight but was unable to try out his propulsion and steering apparatus. He flew for about an hour and a quarter before landing at Bilancourt.

In the next few years there were many attempts at building steering and propulsive mechanisms for balloons, but that there was little understanding of the

François Pilâtre de Rozier and François Laurent lifting off on their historic first flight on 21 November 1783 at Château de la Muette.

principles is clear from the numerous plans for balloons with sails – the balloon moves with the air around it, so a sail makes no difference.

The roll-call of early French balloonists is long: Xavier de Maistre and Brun, Coustard de Massy and Mouchet, Abbot Carnus and Louchet, Mme Thible – the first woman balloonist – and Fleurant, Bremond and Mazet to name but a few, and all in 1784. Some of these balloons carried enormous burners and there were few experienced pilots: the wonder is that there was no fatal accident.

Public enthusiasm for balloon flights was immense and there was little tolerance of failure; an aborted ascent at Bordeaux caused a riot during which several people were killed.

On 19 January 1784 Joseph Montgolfier, Pilâtre de Rozier, the Prince of Ligne, the Counts of Laurençin, Dampierre and Porte d'Anglefort, and an unknown M Fontaine who leapt aboard at the moment of launch, ascended in a balloon constructed of lightweight cloth lined with paper with a capacity of 800,000 cubic feet

Following their trouble-free first flight in a hydrogen balloon, Robert climbs out at Nesles before Charles takes off again to observe a second sunset.

Descente de la Machine Aérostatique, des Srs Charles et Robert.

(226,500 cubic metres) – a record for those days. It rose to 3000 feet (914 m), but the envelope was weak and developed a large tear and the flight lasted only a quarter of an hour.

Soon manned balloons were being built and launched in many countries: Italy, Britain, Austria and Spain in 1784; Germany in 1785 and Blanchard doing the rounds of Holland and Belgium 1785, Switzerland 1788, Poland and Austro-Hungary 1789, and the United States in 1793.

In 1785 Pilâtre de Rozier discovered the folly of having a flame near a hydrogen balloon when he attempted to cross the English Channel under a hydrogen balloon with a small hot-air balloon beneath it. His idea was that the hot-air balloon made of goatskin would be used to alter the altitude so as to make use of favourable air currents. Inevitably, the burner set the gas bag alight; it burnt very rapidly and the contraption fell to earth killing de Rozier instantly and fatally injuring his collaborator in the flight, Pierre-Ange Romain. They achieved the distinction of being the first ballooning fatalities.

Moments before its first ascent from the Champs de Mars, Blanchard's balloon is attacked by Dupont du Chambon. Despite damage to the propulsion and steering apparatus, Blanchard flew for 75 minutes.

Until the airship was developed in the mid-19th century, balloons were the only flying machines. However, they remained more or less unchanged during that time and their dreamed-of potential was never realized because there were few ways of improving the basic design, especially of the more practical hydrogen balloon. However they did enable the atmosphere to be studied extensively, and balloonists developed instruments such as the altimeter, and techniques such as cross-country navigation, that later proved useful in fixed-wing flight.

One area in which the 19th-century balloon was useful was the study of the upper atmosphere. Probably the first ascent for scientific purposes was in 1803 when two daring investigators, Robertson and Lhoest, ascended to 25,500 feet (7770 m). During their flight they recorded the temperature at altitude (19.6F; -7C), and ascertained that glass and wax would not hold static electricity when rubbed. They also observed that a battery lost much of its power (probably because of

Blanchard's original design for a human-powered flying machine included musical accompaniment.

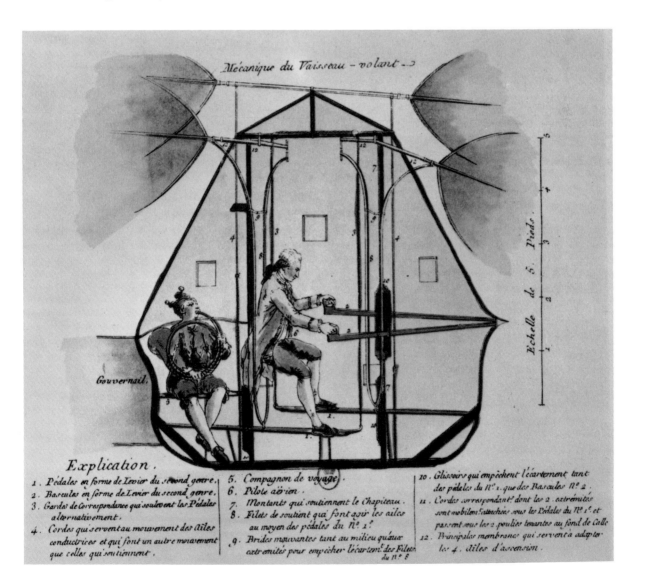

Left
Various ideas were proposed for balloon propulsion, including bird power, sails, oars, and altering the angle of elongated balloons so as to ascend and descend in a particular direction.

Right
The first ballooning fatalities: François Pilâtre de Rozier and Pierre-Ange Romain learning the hard way that hydrogen is highly flammable.

the low temperature) and that sound travelled less easily at altitude. They also tried to perform an experiment to determine the boiling point of water at high altitude, but it seems that Robertson broke the thermometer by putting it into the fire instead of the water. They observed that they felt sleepy, were short of breath, and felt lethargic in a similar manner to those who climbed high mountains.

Another couple of early high-altitude experimenters were Biot and Gay-Lussac. In 1804 they made an ascent to conduct various experiments with birds and insects. Gay-Lussac later went up on his own to 23,000 feet where he took samples of the atmosphere; these were tested and found to have the same proportion of oxygen as the air at ground level.

On 5 September 1862 James Glaisher and Henry

Coxwell rose to an estimated 37,000 feet (11,300 m) – higher than anyone had ever been before. At 29,000 feet (8840 m) they were experiencing paralysis and partial loss of consciousness, but continued to ascend as their plan was to go as high as possible. The account of the flight above this level is sketchy as the two seem to have been lapsing in and out of consciousness; fortunately Coxwell managed to pull the valve line with his teeth (his hands being paralysed) to release gas and descend, whereupon they recovered fully. They also released pigeons at different altitudes, some of which survived, while others perished.

The two big problems of lighter-than-air flight were propulsion and steering. Until they were resolved the balloon for the most part remained a hobby for the rich and a fairground attraction for the masses, rather than a practical vehicle for carrying passengers or freight. Despite the lack of control various firsts were achieved – the first aerial Channel crossing in 1785, the first

An early 19th century proposal for the military use of balloons – a French invasion of England. The English are retaliating with anti-balloon man-carrying kites.

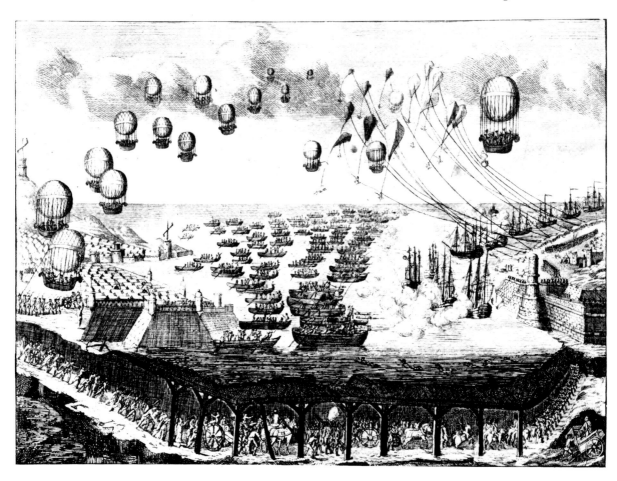

Balloons were used for observation during the US Civil War – this one is being inflated by a mobile hydrogen generator before the Battle of Fair Oaks in May 1862.

aerial crossing of the Adriatic in 1804 and the first aerial crossing of the Alps in 1849. Additionally, the balloon proved very useful when tethered as an observation platform during military campaigns – for example at the Battle of Fair Oaks (1862) during the US Civil War. They were used at the siege of Paris (1870–71) to carry mail from the city over the heads of the Prussians; they also sent carrier pigeons which were intended to bring back news on microfilm – but out of 400 birds, only 57 returned. The use of balloons during the siege was a great success, despite two problems: manufacturing a continual supply of balloons (as they couldn't return); and training balloon pilots (as they couldn't return either). Attempts were made to try and fly back to the city and, had the campaign lasted, enough experience would doubtless have been gained for them to have been successful.

Airships

Many methods were tried to overcome the lack of control in balloons – paddles, wings, wheels, oars, rudders and sails – but they all suffered from similar flaws. Sails were no use because there is no relative wind on a free balloon, and the others mainly relied on the strength of the people aboard, which was hopelessly inadequate as a propulsive force. Another disadvantage was that the cross-section the balloon presented was the same all round.

General Meusnier is credited with the airship shape that evolved to provide a clear direction of travel. With this shape it is possible to present a small cross section while having a large volume of gas (and hence great lifting power). Meusnier is also credited with the idea of having an air bag within the gas envelope which could be altered in volume to keep the gas bag rigid. Unfortunately, he was killed in 1786 before he had a chance to try out his ideas and balloons then lapsed into things of amusement until the airship concept began to bear fruit in the mid-1800s and developed as a viable passenger and freight carrying platform.

Once the airship shape had been established, the problem then was to provide a propulsion unit of sufficient power and lightness.

The honour of designing the first successful man-carrying airship fell to Henri Giffard (1825–1882). It

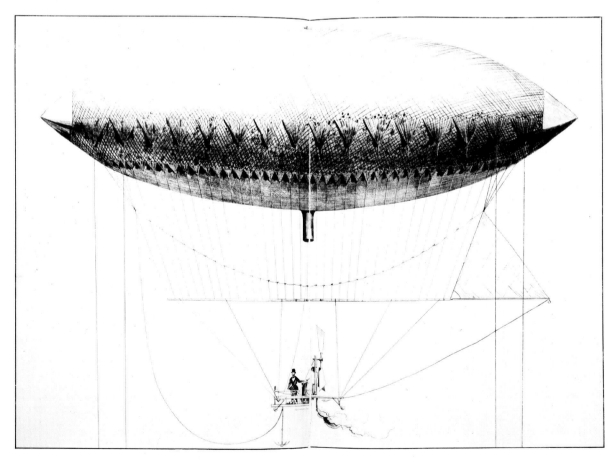

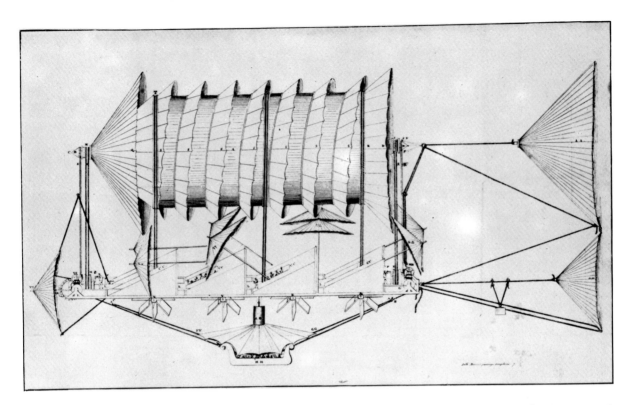

Just two of the many ideas for using a screw to propel an airship. Pierre Ferrand's design of 1835 (above) has a crew on the upper deck to power the main airscrew and control propellers, while passengers in the gondola enjoy the trip. J B J Lassie had different ideas for the passengers of his Aërial Treadmill (below), proposing they should help the crew, who were furiously running round the inside, by pumping air in or out to alter the ship's buoyancy.

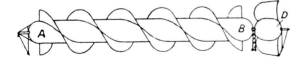

Left
Henri Giffard's steam-powered airship of 1852.

was powered by a 3 hp steam engine driving a propeller 12 feet (3.7 m) in diameter, behind which was a triangular rudder to provide steering. The chimney from the engine was inverted to minimize the risk of igniting the hydrogen. It flew 17 miles (27.4 km) at 5 mph (8 kph) near Paris on 24 September 1852, but was unable to make headway into the wind. It was a start, but it lacked the performance to be a useful vehicle. Giffard told a friend he was dissatisfied with the performance of his machine and did not try it again, instead putting his efforts into a new design.

Gaston and Albert Tissandier made a similar shaped balloon in 1883 powered by an electric motor which could hold its own in a wind of just under 7 mph (11 kph).

The first practical airship was *La France*, built by Captain Charles Renard and Captain Arthur Krebs. It was driven by a 9 hp electric motor and flew several journeys near Paris during August 1884, on most occasions returning to the same point from which it had started – an achievement unheard of until then.

To stimulate the development of practical airships, a Monsieur Deutsch offered a prize equivalent to £4,000 to the first person to take off from the grounds of the

The Tissandier brothers' electrically-powered airship shortly before its flight on 8 October 1883.

Aero Club at Saint Cloud, fly to and round the Eiffel Tower four miles (6.5 km) distant, and then return to the Aero Club within thirty minutes. A Brazilian millionaire, Alberto Santos-Dumont (1873–1932), who lived in France and had taken up airship design and piloting with enormous enthusiasm, won the prize in his Santos-Dumont Number 6 in 1901, having accumulated much experience through building and flying five earlier airship designs. Santos-Dumont continued building and flying airships until he got to number 14. He then went on to make the first powered fixed-wing flight in Europe and continued work in this area with that same single-mindedness with which he had pursued airships.

Two different types evolved: pressure airships and rigid airships. Pressure airships, like the early types, were small and kept in shape by the pressure of the gas within, the shape of the envelope and the containment arrangement around the envelope from which the basket was suspended. Rigid airships kept their shape because they had a rigid framework over which a covering was attached. Inside the frame were a number of gasbags which could be altered in volume to control the altitude of the vessel, as well as other equipment. Engines and passenger gondolas were attached to the frame but hung outside it. Because of their rigidity these airships grew to very large sizes before their eventual demise on safety grounds. The Germans pioneered the rigid airships, which acquired the nickname Zeppelins after Count Ferdinand von Zeppelin (1838–1917) who launched his first design from the Bodensee in 1900. Later Zeppelins were used for passenger carrying as well as bombing London during the First World War.

Right
Gaston Tissandier (left) and his brother Albert in the
basket of their airship, which had to be strong
enough to carry two heavy banks of electric batteries.

Charles Renard and Arthur Krebs' *La France*, the
first airship to fly a closed circuit.

Alberto Santos-Dumont rounding the Eiffel Tower on his way to winning the Deutsch Prize in 1901.

Above and right above
Accidents to the Santos-Dumont 5 (right) and 6 (opposite above) did little to dampen the enthusiasm for flight of Alberto Santos-Dumont, a Brazilian who became a pioneer of fixed-wing flight in Europe.

Right below
The first Zeppelin moored in its floating, movable hangar on the Bodensee.

The Parachute

The first person to try a parachute was an architect, Fauste Veranzio, who in 1617 descended from a tower in Venice under a design he had built himself after Leonardo's idea. He is said to have made a number of descents before giving up the 'sport', perhaps under persuasion from family or friends, perhaps because the experience became more frightening than it was worth once he had done it a few times. Without being able to improve the performance of the parachute, and having nothing higher than a tower to jump from, it would seem reasonable to suppose that he tired of his device fairly rapidly.

In 1797 André-Jacques Garnerin made the first parachute descent from a balloon at a height of 3,000 feet (914 m).

The parachute was both a safety device to escape from a damaged balloon in an emergency, and the next step of an adventurous person who had tired of the thrill of flight. Garnerin's descent was extremely brave for, though he had tried experiments with weights and animals before risking his own life, there could be no going back if it went wrong. Garnerin subsequently made many jumps, including one from 8,000 feet (2440 m) over London during which the parachute took longer than usual to open, and must have given the intrepid experimenter some anxious moments.

Leonardo da Vinci's parachute, said to have inspired Fauste Veranzio's design.

A prisoner escaping using a parachute made from a sheet in the 1639 novel *Ariane* by Des Maretz.

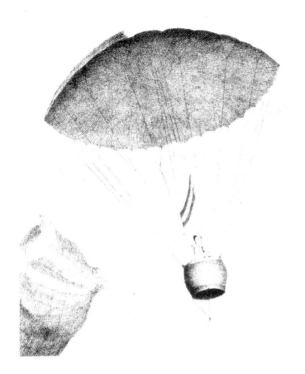

André-Jacques Garnerin's first descent by parachute from a balloon.

Three stages of Robert Cocking's discovery that scaling working models up to full size does not always bring about the desired result.

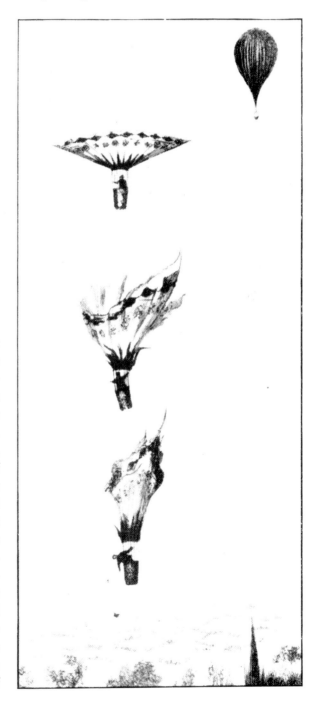

One not so lucky was an English watercolour painter, Robert Cocking. In 1837 he picked up an idea for a stable parachute from the aeronautical experimenter Sir George Cayley. The problem with the umbrella type was that it tended to swing violently, as the air trapped beneath spilled out from the edges. Cayley's stable design was of an inverted cone shape, which righted itself under oscillation by the action of the increased air pressure on its lower side. Cocking's embodiment of this design was made of material held in shape by rods, from which was suspended a basket for the parachutist to ride in. Unfortunately it was structurally unsound; the air flowing past it as it descended forced it to collapse, and the hapless Mr Cocking met his death. A trial run with a sandbag for weight would have harmlessly pointed out this structural flaw, and Cocking must have been either supremely confident or incredibly stupid not to have tested his device first. The problem of swinging parachutes was subsequently solved by putting a hole at the apex of

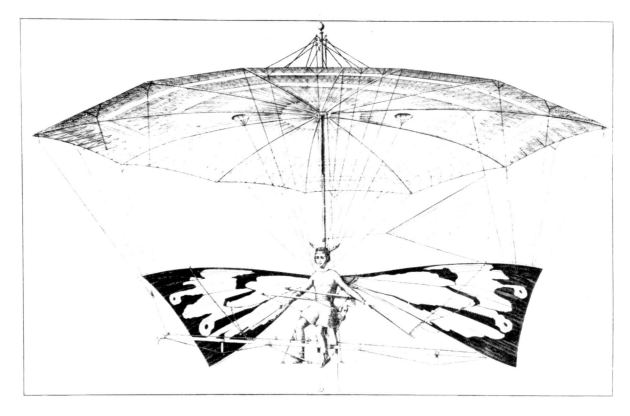

François Letur's steerable parachute.

the canopy through which the trapped air could escape.

Around 1852, François Letur demonstrated a steerable parachute which he flew from a balloon to the ground. It is not clear if he was attempting to develop a useful flying machine, a safety device or a sport. Whatever his intention, it was brought to a premature end a couple of years later when the wind drove him into some trees and he was fatally injured.

In 1864 Vincent de Groof, a Belgian, devised a similar device to Letur's and spent the following 10 years 'perfecting' his design. It had two 24-foot (7m) wings and a 20-foot (6m) tail, each of which could be controlled in flight. The idea was to parachute from a balloon in a predetermined direction. Unfortunately for de Groof, he had omitted to provide a mechanical stop to limit the upward swing of the wings – presumably thinking that the strength of his arms would be enough. This was not the case though, and when he was released from a balloon for the first time in July 1874 over London, the wings folded above him like a butterfly's and he crashed to the ground and was killed. He didn't heed the hard-learned lesson of Cocking, and paid the price.

In the 1880s 'Professor' Baldwin, an American aeronaut, became well known for his daring parachute jumps. The picture shows one such jump he made in 1888 at Alexandra Palace in London where he ascended to 7000 feet beneath a balloon before sliding off the rope seat and descending under the parachute – an incredibly brave thing to do given the rudimentary nature of his apparatus.

After the likes of Cocking, Letur and de Groof, parachutists accepted the limitations of the idea and the basic shape of the parachute. As they have developed in their workable form, they have saved countless lives of those in stricken aircraft, as well as causing the deaths of some of those trying the experience out as a sport.

Below
Vincent de Groof investigating the flying properties of his steerable parachute on its maiden, and last, flight. The balloon rose to a great height unencumbered by the weight of de Groof and his machine.

'Professor' Baldwin, demonstrating a vice-like grip, prepares to land after descending 7000 feet (2,135 m).

Ornithopters

Because birds fly by flapping their wings, it was long thought by many that this was the only successful way to fly. Presumably the would-be aviators of old thought that God must have equipped birds with the best method of flight there was, and who were they to look for other possible solutions? What they failed to recognize was the growing inefficiency of the method as the size of the body increased, and the fact that nature could not develop the propeller as we know it today for the want of a joint able to rotate continuously. It did take quite a long time for people to see the limitation of the method. Apart from the bird men, some of whom we mentioned earlier, there are some amusing examples from the last century of those who sought to solve the problem of flight with ornithopters.

At the beginning of the 19th century, Count Adolphe de Lambertye proposed a military flying machine – L'Aerienne – raised by a pair of flapping wings and propelled by another pair. The wings were to be hand operated by the crew, which Lambertye optimistically set at nine. As well as a deck for the men powering the wings, the machine had an upper observation deck, *and* a lower rest deck! Communication between the machine and the ground was effected by a man-powered helicopter, normally suspended underneath. Looking at the picture, it's interesting to note that the view from the observation deck would have been obstructed by the wings, while those on the rest deck would have had a clear view.

The helicopter beneath Lambertye's flying machine bears a strong similarity to Leonardo's design.

In 1809 Jacob Degen, a clockmaker from Vienna, flew with a pair of flapping umbrella-like wings powered by his arms. There was a catch to his trick as he was attached to a small hydrogen balloon capable of lifting most of his weight, so he only had to produce a small amount of extra lift with his apparatus. The idea was that the wings could be used to provide directional thrust and drag the balloon along. In 1812 Degen exhibited his invention in Paris and gave three public demonstrations. None of these was particularly impressive because on each occasion he was blown away by the wind. Finally, the disappointed spectators attacked him, beat him up and smashed his machine. Despite the balloon being there for all to see he was reported as having flown under his own power, and

Jacob Degen's flapping wings, without the hydrogen balloon that provided most of the lift.

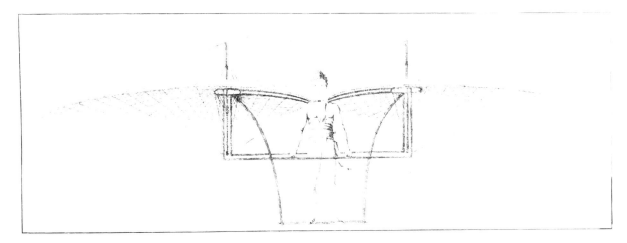

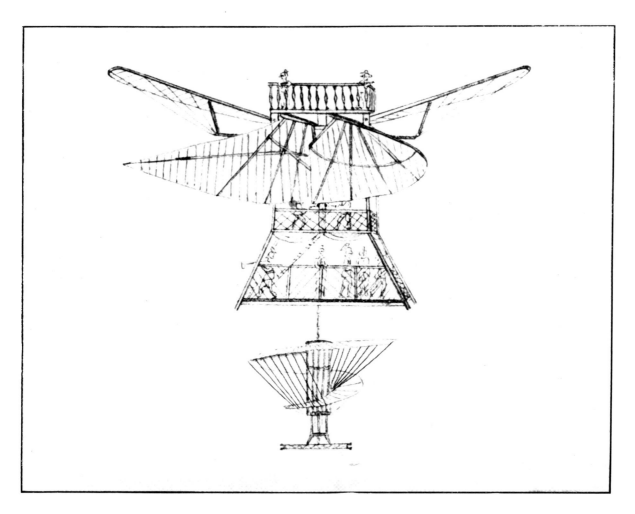

Count Adolphe de Lambertye's aerial observation machine, with communication helicopter slung beneath..

his worthless efforts may have indirectly set back the cause of powered flight by several decades.

Hureau de Villeneuve, the permanent secretary of the French Aeronautical Society, experimented with ornithopters for 25 years from the mid 1860s and made some 300 experimental flying models which convinced him that flapping wings were the best way to achieve flight. He built a huge steam-powered ornithopter in the form of a bat with a 50 foot (15.2m) wingspan. In the knowledge that it would definitely not fly if a complete steam engine was aboard to power it, de Villeneuve used a ground-based boiler (with its fuel and water) to feed steam via a flexible hose to the moving parts of an engine fixed to the machine. With de Villeneuve standing on his contraption, the steam was turned on and the thing flapped itself into the air. Alarmed that he might fly beyond the reach of the hose if he rose too high, de Villeneuve shut off the steam and his machine crashed to the ground and broke. The inventor had seen the potential of his design and decided not to scrap it, or to rebuild it immediately, but to wait until a sufficiently light steam engine was developed before resurrecting his experiment – presumably he was still waiting when he died. Unfortunately, there is no known picture of the flight.

Despite the failure of the full-size machines, many model ornithopters flew with varying degrees of success. Gustave Trouvé devised a flying model bird consisting of two sealed curved tubes set next to one another. Attached to each end of the tubes were wings.

Gustave Trouvé's cartridge-powered model bird.

When compressed gas was fed into the tubes, they tended to straighten; when the gas was released, the tubes returned to their original curve. This effect produced a flapping movement of the wings, by alternately supplying and releasing the gas. The gas came from twelve cartridges in a revolver. To start the bird in flight, it was suspended from a frame by two threads. One thread – attached so that the bird hung level – held the hammer of the revolver back from the first cartridge; the other held the bird so that the first thread was drawn away from the vertical. When the second thread was released, the bird swung forward taking the suspending thread through a flame which burnt through it. This also released the hammer of the revolver, which set the first cartridge off, imparting an initial flap to the wings. The next cartridge was advanced within the revolver by the movement of the curved tubes, and when they reached their initial position the next cartridge was fired. It is claimed that the bird could fly 80 yards (73m). Trouvé's proposal to scale the machine up to carry people was never put into action.

In the 1870s Alphonse Pénaud (1850–1880) demonstrated several small mechanical helicopters and orni-

The launch sequence of Trouvé's bird: the candle, A, burnt through the thread, releasing the bird which swung forward so that the suspension cord was burnt by the blow-pipe flame, B.

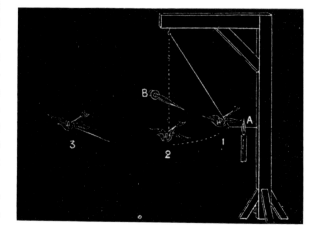

thopters powered by rubber bands. These flew successfully for short distances, but Pénaud understood the limitations of the technique and went on to design a fixed-wing plane.

Lawrence Hargrave (1850–1915), an Australian engineer, built some 16 successful flapping-wing models powered at first by rubber bands and clockwork mechanisms, and later by compressed-air engines. He believed that, as a means of propulsion, flapping wings were just as effective as a propeller, and had the advantage that they weren't damaged by the ground when the machine landed. Once he had demonstrated to his satisfaction that large flapping-wing models would fly, he designed and constructed a light steam engine which he used to power two more flapping-wing models. He did not believe that full-size ornithopters would work, but that flapping wings would be used to propel fixed-wing aeroplanes, so he then turned his attention to the study of fixed-wing aerodynamics, coming up with the box-kite structure that influenced early aircraft design. He was convinced powered flight would come about, but discontinued his own work – possibly because he was tired of being treated as a crank, for he remarked: 'The people of Sydney who can speak of my work without a smile are very scarce; it is doubtless the same with American workers. I know that success is dead sure to come, and therefore do not waste time and words in trying to convince unbelievers.'

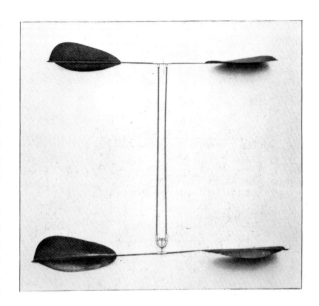

Alphonse Pénaud's early helicopter model. The propellers were wound in opposite directions, twisting the flexible linkage between them. Once released, the linkage unwound and drove the model through the air.

Following his simple helicopter models, Pénaud designed this model bird, powered by rubber bands, in 1874.

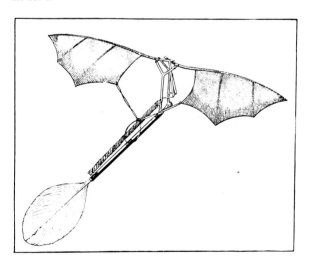

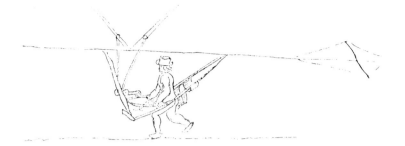

An ornithopter design by Sir George Cayley. It's hard to believe he had any hope that it would fly.

One of Lawrence Hargrave's compressed-air-powered model ornithopters, still attached to its charging pump. Compressed air was held in the cylindrical body, and powered a tiny motor at the base of the two flappers. Additional in-flight lift was supplied by the wings on either side of the body.

Fixed-Wing Flight

The father of fixed-wing flight was a British inventor, Sir George Cayley (1773–1857), who was rich enough to devote a good deal of time and money to the study of aeronautics. He first experimented in 1796 with a bow-powered helicopter similar to that of Launoy and Bienvenue. It may be supposed that the success of the propeller action of his model would have led him to use propellers for driving his aeroplane designs, but for most of his life he remained faithful to the idea of flappers to provide propulsive force. He did however realize early on that the lift supplied by a wing was entirely separate from thrust derived from flapping, which is the principle of the ornithopter.

In 1804 he made his first model glider, which had a kite-like main wing and a cruciform tail attached to the body by a universal joint so that it could act as an adjustable elevator and rudder. It was the first modern-configuration aeroplane in history. In 1809 he built the first successful full-size glider, of which he wrote: 'It was very beautiful to see this noble white bird sail majestically from the top of a hill to any given point of the plain below it, according to the set of its rudder, merely by its own weight...' he also tried tentative experiments in human flight '...when any person ran forward in it, with his full speed, taking advantage of a gentle breeze in front, it would bear upward so

Though thought of as the father of fixed-wing flight, Cayley spent a great deal of time designing propulsion equipment for airships – in this case propellers and flappers.

A model of Cayley's convertiplane – Robert Taylor's idea, though Cayley gave him no credit.

strongly as scarcely to allow him to touch the ground; and it would frequently lift him up, and convey him several yards together.'

However, Cayley could see no use for gliders, and devoted most of his efforts to powered flight, which would provide transport for people and freight. Sadly, because he was pre-occupied with flapper propulsion, he never got anywhere near a successful design, though over the years he produced idea after idea for ornithopters and compound flying machines (fixed wings and flapper propulsion).

Perhaps the greatest hindrance to Cayley's realisation that flappers would never be good enough was the clockmaker Degen. In 1809 a report that Cayley read described Degen's work thus: 'M. Degen, a watchmaker of Vienna, has invented a machine, by which a person may rise into the air. It is formed of two parachutes, of taffeta, which may be folded up or extended at pleasure; and the person who moves them is placed in the centre. M. Degen has made several public

experiments, and rose to the height of fifty-four feet, flying in various directions, with the celerity of a bird. A subscription has been opened at Vienna, to enable the inventor to prosecute his discoveries.' There was no mention of the balloon that bore most of the weight, and Cayley believed up to his death that Degen had achieved human-powered flapping flight.

In 1809–10 Cayley wrote a three-part paper, *On Aerial Navigation*, which was the first treatise in history on both theoretical and practical aerodynamics. Among other things he wrote about aerofoil shapes, directional control, and stability. Of particular interest is the design of a parachute he made, which prevented the violent oscillations of the Garnerin type. It consisted of an inverted cone instead of an umbrella shape. The stability came from the fact that if it swayed, air pressure would be greater on the down-swinging side and would tend to push it upright again. He made a paper model weighted at its apex with lead, to prove his theory. It worked. Unfortunately, as Cocking found

Constructional detail from Henson's patent of 1842 (no 9478).

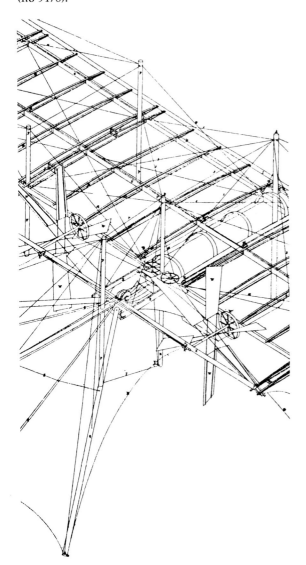

out, there were structural problems in translating the idea to full-size.

In 1816–17 he concerned himself with airship design, and touched on the idea of the rigid airship with the comment that his first design would be 'kept to its shape by light poles attached to it'. As with his fixed-wing designs, it was his propulsion methods that let him down, with such ideas as releasing the airship from the ground at an angle so that it would sail off in the required direction; having sails wafted by a steam engine; or his favourite – flapper propulsion. On his third design he alighted on the idea of propellers.

In 1843 Cayley produced a design for a 'convertiplane' which was designed to take off vertically using horizontal fans which would then flatten to become wings. Propulsion was provided by two pusher airscrews. However, though Cayley claimed the convertiplane as his own brainchild, a man from the U S, Robert Taylor, had written to Cayley proposing the idea and seeking his opinion. The letter remained undiscovered in Cayley's archives for many years.

Between 1849 and 1853 Cayley again turned his attention to gliders. He built one which was reported to have carried a boy aloft for a few yards, as well as his famous coachman-carrying glider of 1853. In this he persuaded one of his servants – reputedly his coachman – to fly across a valley behind his home, Brompton Hall. The machine flew across the valley and crashed into the other side, where the shaken coachman struggled out, saying: 'Please, Sir George, I wish to give notice, I was hired to drive and not to fly.'

Cayley did little more practical work in aeronautics, though his mind remained active on the subject until his death in 1857. Throughout his life, Cayley worked to bring powered flight about, convinced that it would be achieved one day. But his many flapping designs hid his real contribution to aeronautics; his most important work – his triple paper of 1809–10 – lay ignored until the last decade of the 19th century when it was read by such pioneers as Lilienthal, Chanute and the Wright Brothers.

William Samuel Henson (1805–1888) from Chard in Somerset, patented an aircraft design in 1842. It incorporated movable rudder and elevator control surfaces, a cabin for carrying passengers and was driven by two propellers powered by a steam engine. In 1843 with his friend John Stringfellow (1799–1883) and two others, he attempted to raise capital to fund *The Aerial Steam Transit Company*. With not so much as a working model of his design, and a prospectus full of references to the uncertainty of success, there were no subscribers to the shares and the idea folded.

Henson and Stringfellow decided to fund their own development work and built a model from Henson's patent design in 1844. It had a 20-foot (6m) wingspan and weighed about 28 lbs (13kg). It was far too big to fly indoors so they had to conduct tests outdoors. Sensitive to the comments of spectators, they conducted trials at night, but the damp ground soaked the flimsy model and it never flew. Soon afterwards, Henson emigrated to America.

Stringfellow continued work on his own and built a smaller steam-powered monoplane similar to Henson's original design. It had a 10-foot (3m) wingspan and weighed about six lbs (2.7kg). It was just small enough to fly indoors, launched down a 20-foot (6m) wire so that it could build up speed. When it reached

Henson's patent showing the internal structure of the wings, deep body shape, and twin pusher propellers.

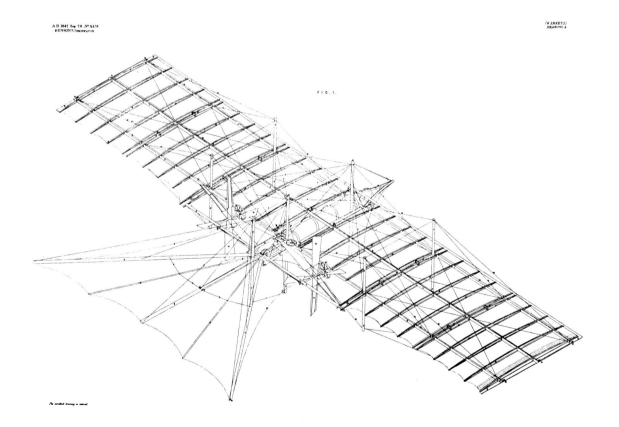

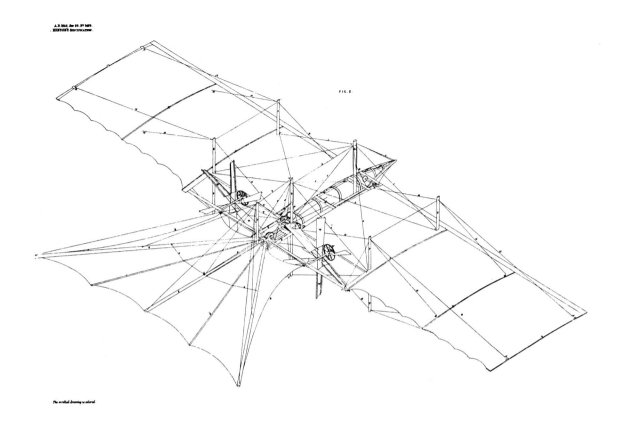

Henson's design with the wing covered.

the end of the wire it flew on, gaining height before being caught in a sheet of canvas supended at the far end of the room. At a demonstration in London it flew 120 feet (37m). This was the first steam-powered flying model that actually flew, but it was so close to the limits of the technology and understanding of the time that Stringfellow could see no possible improvements, and since he had achieved little recognition and spent quite a bit of money, he decided not to continue. In 1868 he built a steam-powered model triplane but it never flew.

Captain Jean-Marie Le Bris, a French sailor, was fired with enthusiasm to build a flying machine, inspired by the effortless way albatrosses flew. His first experiment consisted of killing one of these birds: 'I took the wing of the albatross and exposed it to the breeze; and lo! in spite of me it drew forward into the wind; notwithstanding my resistance it tended to rise. Thus I had discovered the secret of the bird! I comprehended the whole mystery of flight.' Well hardly, but he real-

Stringfellow's steam-powered monoplane model –
the first of its kind to fly.

Left
An optimistic artist's impression of two of Henson's
craft flying over Dover.

ized that the shape of the wing gave it lift when wind
blew over it.

In 1855, he built a machine with the form of the bird
very much in mind; it had a body like a canoe, a wing
span of 50 feet (15.2 m), a hinged tail which could be
controlled by a pedal, and weighed 92 pounds (42 kg).
The front edges of the wings were adjustable in flight
by levers to channel the wind above or below the sur-
face. Le Bris proposed to stand in the craft working the
levers by hand and the tail pedal by foot. His first
experiments consisted of facing the craft into wind, but
not unexpectedly it failed to rise to the occasion. To
provide a stiffer breeze over the wings, Le Bris tied the
craft on to a cart and had it pulled along by a horse.
According to contemporary records, when he felt it
wanted to rise he released a knot so that the craft could
fly free, but it was caught on the cart and so did not
release. Instead, it began to lift the whole cart, and the
horse – relieved of the weight – galloped faster and
faster until the craft broke free and flew up. A length of

rope attached to the machine became wrapped around the horseman and lifted him up too. Le Bris, unaware of the drama below, enjoyed the ascent until he heard the cries of the driver. He then let the craft fly to earth so gently that the driver was uninjured. As soon as the driver's weight was off the rope, the balance of the machine was upset; Le Bris could not sustain the glide and landed heavily, breaking a wing.

Encouraged by his success, Le Bris set up a rig at the edge of a quarry to release his glider from some height, intending to pilot his machine to the quarry floor 100 feet (30 m) below. What he did not take into account was the turbulence of the air blowing over the lip of the quarry, and as he flew down into the invisible mæl-strom, his craft was picked up and dashed to the ground. Le Bris is said to have held on to a part of his craft and, at the point of impact, thrust himself upwards to minimize the shock; unfortunately, a rebounding control lever broke his leg.

His craft wrecked by the quarry crash, Le Bris had no more cash for another experiment and 12 years passed before a public subscription in 1867 provided him with funds to try again. He built a second 'albatross' and ballasted it for un-manned flight after persuasion by his friends who were fearful of his safety. This one flew

The fearless Captain Jean-Marie Le Bris aboard his flying machine. The undercarriage is a cart which was not carried aloft.

Clement Ader's *Avion* with its wings folded (above), in the process of being prepared for 'flight', and ready for take off (below). Ader claimed *Avion* flew before it ran off the testing ground and crashed.

convicingly once, covering about 600 feet, and landing unharmed on rising ground. However, in launching the machine from the top of a slope into a stiff breeze, it was smashed into the ground and broken beyond repair. Never again did Le Bris have the means to continue his experiments, and he was killed in 1872 by some ruffians while on duty as a special constable.

The first person who claimed to have achieved powered flight was the French engineer Clement Ader (1841–1925). He started his aeronautical investigations in about 1872 by constructing an ornithopter which failed miserably, presumably leading him to the conclusion that fixed wings were the way to go. In 1886, after studying the flight of vultures in Algeria, with no practical flying experience on gliders and seemingly little theoretical knowledge of aeronautics, he constructed a powered man-carrying flying machine, *Eole*. It had a bat-like form, a 46 foot (14 m) wingspan, a 25 hp steam engine driving a four-bladed propeller, and weighed 1100 pounds (500 kg). In October 1890 he conducted his first trials, and claimed a flight of 164 feet (50 m). In September 1891 Ader moved *Eole* to the French Military Academy at Satory and is supposed to have flown it over 300 feet (92 m), crashing at the end of his flight. The French military must have seen some potential in his work because they gave him the funds to build another, similar, craft which he called *Avion*. This he tried out in October 1897 on a circular track at Satory. He seems to have been fairly ignorant of the best conditions for flight as he was trying it on a circular track: practical experience would have told him that his best chance of flying would be in a straight line into wind. But Ader had no previous gliding experience; he had only studied the flight of eagles and presumably thought he knew enough about it to leap straight in. This time he and his friends claimed that he

Lilienthal flies his monoplane from his artificial hill near Berlin. His feet are held back to prevent the glider diving.

Lilienthal flying his bi-plane glider.

flew about 1000 yards (915 m) before he crashed, a cross-wind having taken him off the circular track. If he flew at all it was probably a series of hops; it cannot possibly have been a sustained controlled flight, judging by the way the machine lumbered its way towards destruction. At this point the French military must have seen the folly of giving money to someone who did not seem to have much of an idea, and Ader's experiments came to an end.

For many years Ader was held in high regard by Wilbur Wright, who had read of his experiments, and who he counted as one of a group of 'very remarkable men who in the last decade of the 19th century raised studies relating to flying to a point never before attained.' When Wright finally saw *Avion* in 1911, the experience must have burst the bubble of admiration he had for Ader because he wrote to his brother Orville: '...The wings are not fitted with enough ribs to give them any shape or supporting power. The whole machine is most ridiculous.'

The pioneering German glider pilot Otto Lilienthal (1848–1896), began experimenting at the age of 13 by making wings with a frame of willow, covered with canvas to which he and his brother Gustav had sewn goose feathers. He ran downhill flapping his arms with wings attached, but unsurprisingly never achieved flight. Six years later, the brothers began further practical work, experimenting with wings fastened to their backs and moved by their legs in the fashion of swimming, but the Franco-Prussian War (1870–71) interrupted their as yet unsuccessful efforts. They resumed in 1871; Otto realized that all their attempts at flight had failed because of their incomplete knowledge of how the wing worked, so he entered into detailed studies of flight, observing birds and investigating curved wing surfaces. In 1889 he published a work on the subject of gliding flight and began to build gliders. At first he made models; then full-sized craft that would bear his weight, culminating in his No 11 glider, a monoplane with a peeled willow frame over which was stretched a strong cotton fabric. He flew this himself, and offered copies for sale. On this machine he progressed from short gliding flights from a springboard to much longer flights from the top of a 50-foot conical hill which he had had constructed near Berlin with the earth taken from a nearby canal built in 1892. Inside his hill was a cave in which he kept his gliders. The surrounding terrain had the advantage of being completely flat – there were therefore no other hills to create turbulence in the air. All sides being uniform, he could pick whichever side of the cone was into wind on any particular day.

In addition to his monoplane, Lilienthal made a triplane which he flew successfully. His designs were controlled by movements of the pilot's body which altered the centre of gravity as necessary – so called weight-shift control. He was convinced that when power was successfully applied to flight it would be used to flap the wing. To this end he had modified one of his gliders to have flapping wing-tips which were activated by compressed carbon dioxide gas, controlled by a finger-operated valve. Every time he pressed the valve, the moving surfaces made one flap. Lilienthal made more than 2,000 flights in all, eventually

Lilienthal flying above a crowd of spectators near the end of a glide. The convenience of his artificial hill can be gauged by observing the flat terrain in the background.

Sir Hiram Maxim's huge experimental flying machine, *First kite of war*, outside its hangar at Baldwin's Park in 1892, before its first accident prompted Maxim to build the pine safety rail.

killing himself in 1896 when he stalled his glider and crashed to the ground from 50 feet (15 m); he died the following day. Interested in the possibility of soaring flight – using upcurrents of air to prolong the glide he was flying on an unfamiliar hill at the time of the accident. It is possible that he was trying this new site because he thought there were upcurrents caused by wind being deflected upwards by the hill, and was caught out by unfamiliar turbulence. His chief contribution to the development of powered flight was unwittingly to demonstrate that weight-shift control was unsuitable.

In Britain, the problems of flight were vigorously investigated by the Anglo-American experimenter and inventor Hiram Maxim (1840–1916). In 1887 he invented a machine gun, from which he made a con-

siderable amount of money. With this he was able to conduct some large-scale experiments in aeronautics – a subject in which he was extremely interested. He built a huge experimental test rig at Baldwin's Park, Bexley in Kent, consisting of a flying machine and over 1,000 feet (300 m) of track on which to run it. Maxim seems to have been imbued with a desire to turn his inventiveness to destructive uses as he referred to his craft as his *First kite of war*. It had many wings which in total had a lifting area of 6,000 square feet (540 sq m), though they were removable and he never used more than 4,000 square feet (360 sq m) during his trials. It had two two-bladed propellers 17 feet 11 inches (5.5 m) in diameter. The blades had to be provided with stays after they had been found to bend under their own thrust. It was powered by two 180 hp steam engines.

Maxim reckoned the craft would lift 8000 pounds (3630 kg) which was more than enough to cope with the engine, water in the boiler and tank, the fuel, a crew of three and the craft itself. The purpose of this giant set-up was to find out exactly what the supporting power of a plane was when driven through the air at a slight angle from the horizontal. The gauge of the rails on which it ran was nine feet (2.75 m). The craft had wheels that ran along the track; so that it could not fly free, Maxim built a set of wheels weighing one and a half tons (1.5 t), which allowed the machine to rise six inches (15 cm) before their weight was felt. He made a number of runs; on the last, while travelling at about 35 mph (56 kph) with the craft restrained from free flight by the heavy wheels, a sudden gust of wind caught the wings, which momentarily generated enough lift to derail the machine. A second gust of wind then blew it over causing more than £1,000 worth of damage. Maxim dispensed with the heavy wheels and constructed a second set of safety rails to prevent this happening again. These were made of squared pine logs, two feet (60 cm) above the steel track and with a wider gauge. Outrigger wheels ran under them so that, if the craft lifted off, the outrigger wheels would engage the underside of the safety rails and prevent further gain of height.

Maxim tried his new arrangement in 1894. What an impressive sight this whole construction must have been, with over 1,000 feet (300 m) of track and the steaming multi-winged monster with Maxim and a couple of others aboard rumbling along it. After making several runs with the new safety rail in place, Maxim had the machine constrained by a dynamometer to see what the maximum thrust was. With the propellers being driven at full speed, the attachment broke and, with four people aboard, the machine set off down the track quickly reaching more than 40 mph (65 kph). By 600 feet (180 m) all the outrigger wheels were fully engaged on the underside of the safety rail, and at about 900 feet (270 m) one of the rear outriggers folded and the rear of the craft lifted clear of the safety rail. At 1,000 feet (300 m) the left forward wheels came clear of the rail and shortly afterwards the right forward wheel began to destroy the safety rail. In Maxim's own words 'the machine was liberated and floated in the air, giving those on board the sensation of being in a boat.' Steam was shut off and the craft sank to the ground. Maxim had carried out sustained, powered, man-carrying flight, but it was not aerodynamically controlled, and his machine in no way constituted a practical flying machine – as he himself was the first to admit. Maxim never pretended to have

A rear view of Maxim's machine in 1894, after the addition of the safety rail – the outrigger wheels are visible under the left rail. Once out of the hangar, additional wings were fitted, though it never 'flew' with the 6,000 square feet (560 square m) maximum.

reached a practical solution, coming to the correct conclusion that petrol engines would be a better power source. He also recognized that there was a world of difference between his constrained test-rig and a free-flying, controlled aeroplane. 'I think it will therefore be obvious that those who could navigate the air with machines heavier than the air have a task before them which is worthy of their steel,' he wrote, seeming to imply that he was ruling himself out of such a task, perhaps preferring to leave it to younger, bolder men. Unfortunately, diminishing funds, coupled with the loss of the site where his test track was, prevented him from continuing. Perhaps by way of compensation, in 1896 he became the patron of Percy Pilcher (1866–1899) who had been building and flying gliders in Scotland.

Ignoring the likes of Cayley's coachman, Pilcher was Britain's first glider pilot. An engineer, he built model gliders before building a full-sized version – *The Bat* – in 1895. Before he flew it, he went to see Lilienthal who gave him practical advice and let him fly one of his monoplane gliders. When Pilcher returned to Scot-

Percy Pilcher's first glider, *The Bat*, in 1895, with Pilcher holding its nose into the wind so that it flies. The tail plane was added after the original design crashed.

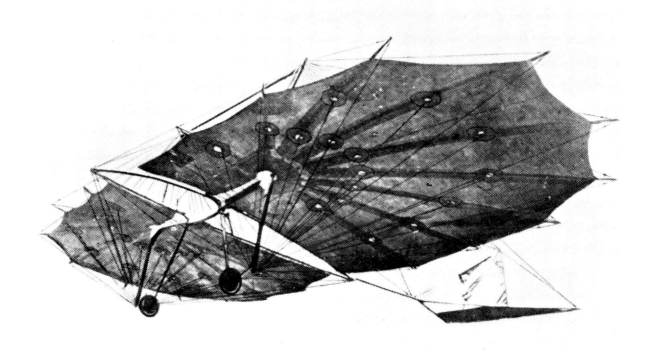

Pilcher's most successful glider, *The Hawk*, built in 1896. Pilcher's favoured configuration of radiating wing supports is clearly visible.

land he was somewhat better prepared to embark on his gliding career. He soon discovered a severe limitation to his design – *The Bat* had no tail-plane (which Lilienthal had urged him to fit) and would not fly. He fitted a tail-plane and some time in June or July 1895 he took off from a hill into a stiff breeze and hovered over the same spot for several seconds before being lowered gently back to the ground again. On his next flight, however, a gust picked up one wing and the glider was broken as it hit the ground. Undaunted, Pilcher rebuilt *The Bat* in a more stable form and had some success in making short glides on it. He next designed and built *The Beetle* which was heavy and unmanageable because it was robust enough to fit an engine to. Perhaps *The Beetle* was heavy as a result of the fragility of *The Bat*. It is interesting to note that, while Lilienthal had much more experience of flying, he was cautious of fitting an engine to one of his craft. Yet Pilcher's second design had an engine in mind; that it was a failure even as a glider demonstrates Pilcher's inexperience.

Following the unmanageable *Beetle*, and a hopelessly fragile third attempt called *The Gull*, Pilcher built his most successful machine, *The Hawk*. All his designs had wings attached to supports radiating from a point. Hargrave attempted to convince Pilcher that it would be better to build a machine in a stronger, more stable box-kite configuration but Pilcher was opposed to that idea on two counts: first, he didn't want the glider to be so stable that it was too difficult for the weight-shift of the pilot to alter its flight path; second, he had an irrational fear of biplanes, thinking that having a wing above his head would decrease the stability of the craft to the point where it would be uncontrollable.

Pilcher didn't see gliding as an end in itself, but rather as preparation for the day when light enough engines would make powered flight a reality; he likened it to learning to ride a bicycle with no crank running down an incline, so that when a bicycle with pedals came along, one could jump on and ride it instantly. The huge, and vital, flaw in his approach was that weight-shift gliders such as his had too small a wing area to support an engine powerful enough to provide the power for flight, and to increase the wing area so that it would support the engine would make the machine impossible to control with weight shift.

During 1898 Pilcher busied himself raising money and designing what he thought would be his powered machine. Called *The Duck*, it was a quadruplane with a pusher propeller, but it was never built, and his eventual design was a triplane along similar lines. He was also building an engine designed by his partner Walter Wilson which produced about four horse power and weighed less than 44 pounds (20kg) with its propeller. This engine had been tested and his triplane was nearing completion when, on 30 September 1899 at Stamford Hall, Market Harborough, Pilcher gave a demonstration of gliding flight on *The Hawk*. Although the weather was bad, Pilcher was keen to give a demonstration to a potential supporter of his venture. To pull him into the air, he was drawn over a level field by two horses, but the glider was wet and would not fly well. Pilcher tried three times, and on his third flight, at about 30 feet (9m), the machine folded and plummeted to the ground. Pilcher was found alive but unconscious in the wreckage. It was thought that he might recover but he died some hours later. He was 34 and had been flying for four years. It is unlikely that Pilcher's triplane would have flown successfully – it has been calculated that the engine would not have produced the power necessary – but since neither the engine nor the plane (or the plans for either) have survived, we will never know. What is beyond doubt is

Drawings from Octave Chanute's multi-plane glider patent of 1897 (no 13,372).

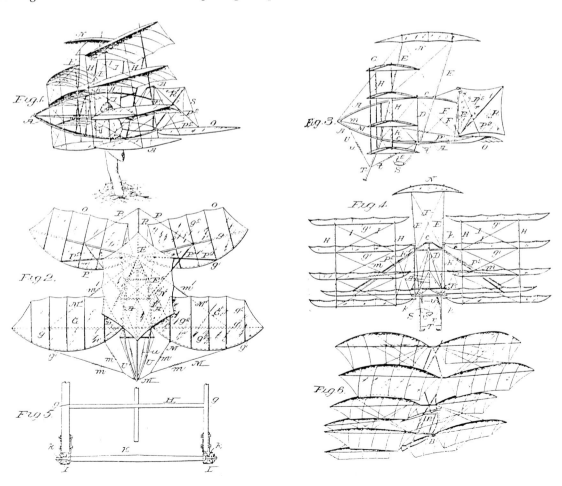

I.—GETTING READY.

III.—OFF.

II.—POISED.

IV.—STOPPING.

Four stages in the flight of Chanute's biplane glider in 1897. The design was little more than a box kite with a tail. The pilot shifted his weight around to keep the wings level.

that Pilcher, despite his brave efforts, was using the wrong approach to control, and contributed little save confirming that weight-shift control was not the way to progress.

Octave Chanute (1832–1910), a civil engineer born in France who later settled in America, contributed a great deal to the solution. He was in correspondence with many of the experimenters around the world, and passed on ideas from one to another – a sort of information exchange. He had long been interested in the problems of flight and had built two types of man-carrying glider which he had tested during 1896 and 1897 with the help of his assistants, Augustus Herring, William Avery, W Paul Butusov and James Ricketts – who did much of the flying. Although they conducted many hundreds of glides, many of them over hundreds of feet, they did not have a single accident. Chanute's gliders were of two types: a multi-plane which

initially had a total of 12 planes, and later a more successful biplane based on Hargrave's box kite. Chanute tried to solve the problems of instability by providing the gliders with wings which moved in response to gusts so as to restore the plane's balance. Later versions of the multi-plane had wings which were moved by foot controls, but the effect was such that moving the left foot forward caused a turn to the right, and *vice versa*, and so control was not instinctive. Chanute never had the idea of reversing the effect of the controls to make it so. With their success, Herring was keen to fit an engine to the multi-plane glider, but Chanute was more restrained, thinking that the control was not sufficient to risk powered flight. In the end, Herring went his own way in 1898 and built a biplane glider with an engine powered by compressed air, which he claimed performed short powered hops into a strong wind. He was never able to demonstrate his powered flight to Chanute, and his machine was destroyed by fire in 1901.

The American astronomer Samuel Pierpoint Langley probably came closest to sustained powered flight without achieving it. While secretary of the Smithsonian Institution in Washington he studied the aerodynamics of wings on a 'whirling table', which used a steam engine to drive an arm around, to the end of which he attached his test material. In the 1890s he built a series of powered models, at first using carbon dioxide gas and then steam. The last two were very successful, making flights of thousands of feet. Langley's models demonstrated the viability of sustained powered flight. However, he did not try a man-carrying machine until asked by the US Army and Navy in 1898 to develop one for military purposes. Langley accepted the invitation and was given $50,000 to pursue the project – though he did the work unpaid. He searched America and Europe for a company that could manufacture an engine powerful enough, yet light enough, for his purposes. In the end, all companies having said it was impossible, it fell to his mechanic Charles Manly to devise a five-cylinder radial engine. This weighed 120 pounds (55 kg) and produced a continuous 50 hp. During the years 1899 to 1903 Langley planned and built his machine which he called The Langley Aerodrome, eschewing the word aeroplane because he thought 'plane' conjured up the picture of a plane surface, whereas his wing was curved. The Aerodrome was steel-framed and weighed 830 pounds (376 kg) with the pilot. It was extremely delicate, and was to be launched from a floating platform so that it had water underneath it in case of an accident in flight. Manley piloted the craft. Unfortunately, during the first launch on 7 October 1903, the front of the aircraft got caught on the launching vessel and the machine was damaged and flew straight into the water. It was repaired and tried again on 8 December, but this time the rear of the machine caught during take-off and the machine was again damaged. While a recovery party was set up it became dark, and during the confusion of trying to recover the wreckage from the water, an enthusiastic tug attached a rope to a wrong part of the aircraft and pulled it in half. Unfortunately for Langley the Wright brothers flew nine days later. Langley had always insisted on secrecy for his work because it was for the army. The press were

Samuel Pierpoint Langley's model *Aerodrome No 5* takes off from its floating launching platform moored on the Potomac River. The *Aerodrome* was steam powered and could fly for over a minute.

therefore somewhat hostile towards him because he would never give them information or show them what he was doing. From their uncomfortable encampments along the mosquito-infested riverside, they were able to observe Langley's failures from a distance and, seizing the opportunity to discredit him, they reported with glee that Langley's machine was totally useless and would never fly. Because of this adverse publicity, Congress refused to fund him further. He was offered commercial capital to develop his machine but, as Manly said, he had 'given his time and best labours to the world without hope of remuneration, and he could not bring himself, at his stage of life, to consent to capitalize his scientific work.'

The first launch of Langley's full size *Aerodrome* on 7 October 1903 with Charles Manley at the controls. Had it not caught on part of the launch apparatus it might well have made the first convincing powered human flight – as it was, it plunged straight into the Potomac.

Langley's *Aerodrome* after the 7 October crash. Although it looks completely wrecked, it was rebuilt in two months, though its second launch was no more successful than the first.

Success

As boys, Wilbur Wright (1867–1912) and his brother Orville (1871–1948), constructed models of flying machines after the designs of Cayley and Pénaud. But their interest in such things was not unusual for children, and as they grew they turned their interests in other directions and settled down in 1892 to run a respectable bicycle manufacture and repair business in Dayton, Ohio. It was the death of Otto Lilienthal four years later that sparked anew their interest in flying machines and stimulated them to investigate the problems involved in control. At the beginning of the Wrights' practical experiments in 1899, having read all they could about the ideas of people such as Cayley, Hargreave, Lilienthal and Chanute, they concluded that aerodynamic control rather than weight-shift was the correct way to control flying machines, a conclusion confirmed in the observation of birds which maintained lateral control by twisting their wing tips. They designed a pair of wings which could be twisted, or 'warped' by the movement of cables running from the wings to a cradle on which the pilot lay. By the action of the pilot moving his body – and thus the frame – from side to side, the wings were twisted and lateral control was effected. The system worked so well with models that they flew as kites, controlling the warping wires from the ground, that the brothers planned to make a full-size glider in 1900. That they had, at that time, no idea of the success that they would achieve, is shown in a letter Wilbur wrote to Octave Chanute in May 1900 in which he said '... I make no secret of my plans for the reason that I believe no financial profit will accrue to the inventor of the first flying machine, and that only those who are willing to give as well as to receive suggestions can hope to link their names with the honour of its discovery. The problem is too great for one man alone and unaided to solve in secret.'

They realized one of the keys to control was practice and so they planned to experiment somewhere that had smooth, turbulence-free hills and guaranteed wind so they could do as much gliding as possible. On advice, they chose a small out-of-the-way place called Kitty Hawk in North Carolina. On arrival, the brothers built their first full-size glider and spent several weeks flying it, much to the interest of the locals. The glider had an elevator at the front which was controlled by a lever independently of the wing warping cradle. They found it very hard to operate the two controls simultaneously; but it worked, which was encouraging.

They learned other valuable, practical lessons, discovering that a permanent prone position was preferable to their planned method of standing up for launching and landing, and lying down only for the flights. The glider would happily land on its belly, sustaining little damage.

That first year, the brothers managed a total of about two minutes' gliding and, encouraged by their success, they planned a bigger glider and another trip for the following year. Wilbur had started a correspondence with Octave Chanute that year, a lot of which concerned aerodynamic theory in which the Wrights were becoming quite expert after constructing a wind tunnel in 1901 to investigate the behaviour of different aerofoil sections. The data they collected helped them to design a better wing shape for their second glider.

For the brothers' 1901 trip they moved to Kill Devil Hills some four miles south of Kitty Hawk. There they built their second glider, which had a wing area of 308 square feet (28 sq m) – larger than the previous year's model, larger indeed than anyone else had dared try. They made many successful glides on the new machine, though the expedition was cut short because of poor weather.

Right
Drawings from the Wright brothers' patent of 1904 (no 6,732) which detailed their method of lateral control by warping the wings long after they had the original idea and successfully tested it.

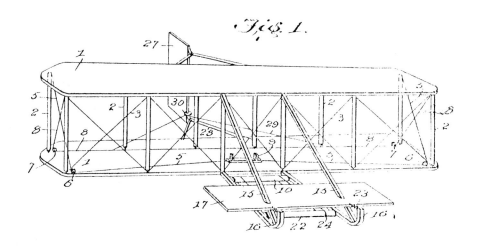

Fig. 1.

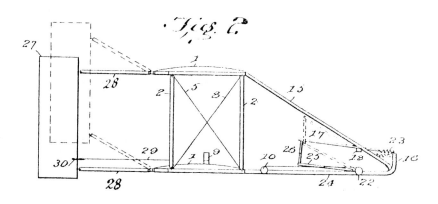

Fig. 2.

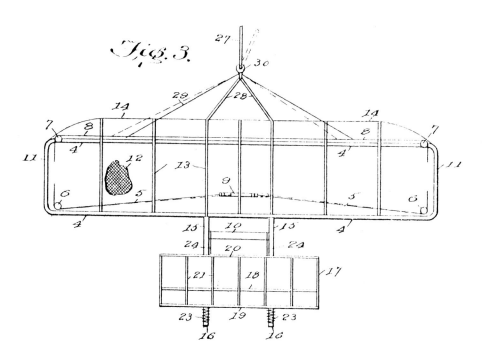

Fig. 3.

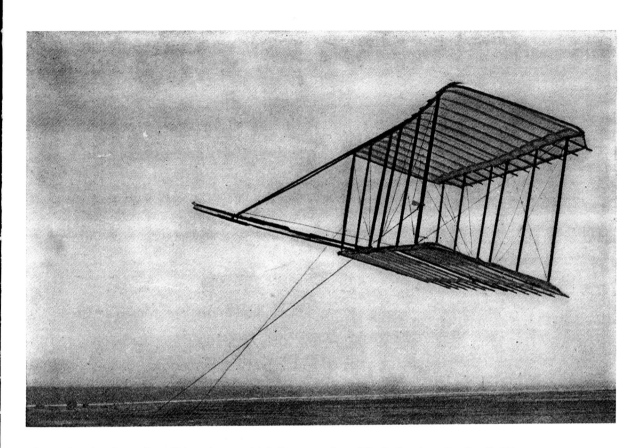

The Wright brothers' first glider of 1900 which they tested as a kite before learning to pilot it.

The Wrights built their third glider at Kill Devil Hills in 1902. It had a vertical tail fin as well as the front elevator. They made nearly one thousand glides, with a longest distance of 622.5 feet (190 m) flown in a time of 26 seconds. Their methods were cautious; first testing their glider as a kite, then flying it from a small hill before gradually working their way up to flying from the largest of the Kill Devil Hills some 100 feet (30 m) high. Wilbur later said: 'For the purpose of reducing the danger to the lowest possible point we usually kept close to the ground. Often a glide of several hundred feet would be made at a height of a few feet or even a few inches sometimes. It was the aim to avoid unnecessary risk. While the high flights were more spectacular, the low ones were fully as valuable for training purposes. Skill comes by the constant repetition of familiar feats rather than by a few over-bold attempts at feats for which the performer is yet poorly prepared.'

After the tests of 1902, the Wrights decided they were ready for powered flight since the problem as they saw it was maintaining control once airborne. They wrote to a number of engine manufacturers, seeking a vibration-free engine of about eight or nine horsepower, and weighing less than 180 pounds (82kg). No one had such an engine so they designed and built their own. It weighed 150 pounds (68kg) and produced 13 horse power.

At the end of September 1903, at Kill Devil Hills, they got their flying hands back in again by gliding the 1902 model while building their *Flyer*.

The *Flyer* was launched from a wheeled carriage which ran along a wooden rail. Chanute was greatly amused by this arrangement, which had cost about

The historic first flight of the *Wright Flyer* on 17 December 1903. Orville Wright is at the controls while Wilbur runs along beside – an indication of the slow ground speed. The position from which the *Flyer* started its take off run is marked by the outline of the wing made by footprints in the sand. While stationary, the *Flyer*'s wing was clamped to the bench at the end of the footprint outline.

four dollars, contrasting it with Langley's multi-thousand-dollar houseboat launching platform which had thus far caused the wreck of his flying machine on the one and only time it had been used.

On 17 December 1903, the Wright brothers became the first men to make controlled flights in a powered heavier-than-air flying machine when they made four flights, each longer than that before, culminating in one of 852 feet (260m) in 59 seconds.

After having numerous ideas, exploring many blind alleys, making countless mistakes, and g.. ing the fragments of knowledge together, mank. had learned enough to take its first faltering hops of powered flight. The methodical way in which the Wrights carried out their investigations laid the foundations for subsequent aeronautical feats, and a multi-billion-dollar industry. Their success did not signal the end of the quest; it was but another milestone – albeit a very important one – on a journey that still continues.